Nutrition

Carbohydrates

by Susan Glick

FOCUS READERS®

BEACON

www.focusreaders.com

Focus Readers is distributed by North Star Editions:
sales@northstareditions.com | 888-417-0195

Produced for Focus Readers by Red Line Editorial.

Photographs ©: Shutterstock Images, cover, 1, 4, 7, 8, 11, 13, 14–15, 16, 19, 20, 22, 25, 27, 29

Library of Congress Cataloging-in-Publication Data
Names: Glick, Susan, author.
Title: Carbohydrates / Susan Glick.
Description: Mendota Heights, MN: Focus Readers, [2025] | Series: Nutrition | Includes bibliographical references and index. | Audience: Grades 2-3
Identifiers: LCCN 2024000401 (print) | LCCN 2024000402 (ebook) | ISBN 9798889981817 (hardcover) | ISBN 9798889982371 (paperback) | ISBN 9798889983477 (pdf) | ISBN 9798889982937 (ebook)
Subjects: LCSH: Carbohydrates in human nutrition--Juvenile literature. | Carbohydrates--Juvenile literature. | Nutrition--Juvenile literature.
Classification: LCC QP701 .G55 2025 (print) | LCC QP701 (ebook) | DDC 613.2/83--dc23/eng/20240201
LC record available at https://lccn.loc.gov/2024000401
LC ebook record available at https://lccn.loc.gov/2024000402

Printed in the United States of America
Mankato, MN
082024

About the Author

Susan Glick lives in Maryland, where she writes books for children.

Table of Contents

Chapter 1

A Healthy Meal

A boy and his mother make a salad together. First, the boy's mom cuts sweet potatoes into small pieces. The boy sprinkles spices on top. Then, his mother puts the potatoes into the oven.

Sweet potatoes have several kinds of carbohydrates.

Meanwhile, the boy makes a dressing. He mixes lime juice and maple syrup. His mother chops up a green pepper and some cilantro. The boy's mother also prepares quinoa.

Next, they place the cooked sweet potatoes and quinoa into a large bowl. The boy mixes in a can

Most carbohydrates are found in plant-based foods.

Quinoa is a grain. It has lots of healthy carbohydrates.

of black beans. He adds the peppers and cilantro. He also stirs in the salad dressing. The tasty meal has many healthy carbohydrates.

Chapter 2

What Are Carbohydrates?

Carbohydrates are often called carbs. They are important for health. That's because carbs give the body **energy**. In fact, they are the body's main energy source.

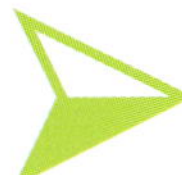

The body uses energy from carbs to exercise and stay active.

Carbs come from different types of food. The body turns most carbs into glucose. Glucose is a sugar. It acts like **fuel** for the body.

There are two groups of carbs. One group is called simple carbs. Simple carbs are found in some natural foods. They are also added to many foods. The body can break down simple carbs quickly. When that happens, glucose enters the blood. That raises a person's **blood sugar**.

Sugars are examples of simple carbs.

The other group is called complex carbs. These are found in many natural foods. The two types of complex carbs are starch and fiber.

The body turns most starches into glucose. However, starches are harder to break down than simple carbs are. So, starches take longer to **digest**. That means starches raise blood sugar for a longer period of time. As a result, the body can use the energy for longer.

Blood sugar levels rise quickly when a person eats simple carbs. But the person may feel tired when blood sugar plummets back down.

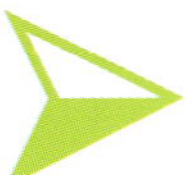

Certain kinds of berries are good sources of fiber.

Fiber is a complex carb that the body cannot digest. It helps control blood sugar. It also helps the body feel full.

Insulin

Insulin is a **hormone**. It helps move glucose into cells. But if the body does not have enough insulin, glucose cannot get into cells. Instead, the glucose builds up in a person's blood. That leads to high levels of blood sugar. Over time, this can harm the body. It may damage the eyes, nerves, **organs**, and more.

Type 1 diabetes happens when the body's cells don't make enough insulin. Type 2 diabetes happens when the body's cells can't use insulin properly. Both types cause high blood sugar.

People with diabetes may have to keep track of their blood sugar levels.

GLUCOMETR
My Glucose
170
mg/dL
1m ago
350
300
250
200
150
100
50
mg/dL

Chapter 3

Types of Carbohydrates

Carbs are found in many types of foods. Foods that have not been **processed** often have lots of **nutrients**. Processed foods are usually much less healthy.

Cookies and pastries are examples of processed foods.

Simple carbs can be found in fruits. Some vegetables also contain simple carbs. That's because fruits and vegetables have natural sugars. Peaches and carrots are two examples. Natural sugars are also in dairy products such as milk and yogurt.

However, people may also get simple carbs from processed foods. Sugar or corn syrup is often added to foods and drinks. These include candy and soda.

Processed foods often contain large amounts of corn syrup.

Complex carbs are usually found in unprocessed foods. For instance, vegetables have lots of fiber. Broccoli and celery are two healthy sources.

Foods with large amounts of fiber are often more filling than low-fiber foods.

Other kinds of foods also have large amounts of fiber. These foods include nuts and beans. They also include whole grains. Whole grains can be found in whole-wheat breads and brown rice. Many fruits contain fiber, too. Apples and berries are healthy sources.

Healthy starches are often found in fiber-rich foods. Lentils and peas are two examples. Whole-grain pasta is another. However, some foods have lots of starch but not much fiber. These include potatoes and corn.

Some foods contain different kinds of carbohydrates. Green peas have fiber, starch, and natural sugars.

Chapter 4

Healthy Choices

Eating healthy carbs is important. The glycemic index can help people make good choices. The glycemic index gives scores to certain foods. These scores show how the foods affect blood sugar.

Foods get scores between 0 and 100 on the glycemic index.

Foods with low scores raise blood sugar slowly. Foods with high scores raise blood sugar quickly. Experts suggest avoiding foods with high scores. Instead, people should choose foods with lower scores. That can help prevent **diseases**.

Often, processed foods have high scores. So, people should replace processed foods with **whole foods**. For example, instant oatmeal has a high score. This meal is made

Besides the glycemic index, the amount of a food eaten and the way it is cooked are also important.

with processed oats. People can eat steel-cut oats instead. Steel-cut oats are whole grains. They have fiber and other nutrients. The body breaks them down more slowly.

Many foods have low scores. They include green vegetables and carrots. They also include most fruits. Kidney beans and chickpeas have low scores, too. So do lentils.

Most people don't eat enough fiber-rich foods. But there are plenty of ways to fix that. Whole grains have more fiber than

Nutrition labels can help people make healthy choices. They show the kinds of carbs in foods.

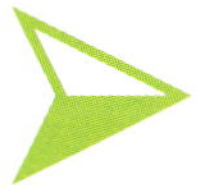

A nutrition label lists the amount of fiber and sugar in foods.

processed grains. Brown rice is an example. Raw vegetables and fruits are also good choices. Snacking on nuts or seeds is another way to get more fiber.

FOCUS ON

Carbohydrates

Write your answers on a separate piece of paper.

1. Write a few sentences describing how the body uses carbohydrates.
2. What is your favorite source of fiber? Why?
3. Which food is a complex carbohydrate?
   A. brown sugar
   B. broccoli
   C. milk
4. What would happen to a person's blood sugar after eating a cookie?
   A. The person's blood sugar would rise.
   B. The person's blood sugar would stay the same.
   C. The person's blood sugar would fall.

5. What does **plummets** mean in this book?

Blood sugar levels rise quickly when a person eats simple carbs. But the person may feel tired when blood sugar ***plummets*** *back down.*

- A. hardens
- B. cools
- C. falls

6. What does **products** mean in this book?

Natural sugars are also in dairy ***products*** *such as milk and yogurt.*

- A. unhealthy foods
- B. things people can buy
- C. kinds of nutrients

Answer key on page 32.

Glossary

blood sugar
The amount of glucose in a person's blood.

digest
To break down food so it can be used by the body.

diseases
Illnesses or sicknesses.

energy
The ability to do work.

fuel
Something that can be used to produce energy.

hormone
A chemical that sends messages to cells and body parts.

nutrients
Substances that living things need to stay strong and healthy.

organs
Sets of tissues that have specific jobs in the body.

processed
When food is changed by adding something to it or preparing it in a certain way.

whole foods
Foods that have not been processed.

To Learn More

BOOKS

Koster, Gloria. *Grains Are Good for You!* North Mankato, MN: Pebble, 2023.

Rea, Amy C. *Carbohydrates as Necessary Nutrients.* Minneapolis: Abdo Publishing, 2023.

Rebman, Nick. *Earth-Friendly Eating*. Mendota Heights, MN: Focus Readers, 2022.

NOTE TO EDUCATORS

Visit **www.focusreaders.com** to find lesson plans, activities, links, and other resources related to this title.

Index

Answer Key: 1. Answers will vary; **2.** Answers will vary; **3.** B; **4.** A; **5.** C; **6.** B